# Angel Writings

# Angel Writings

written through

## Nini Finnegan

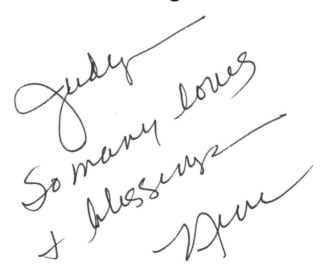

Mill City Press, Inc.
212 3rd Avenue North, Suite 570
Minneapolis, MN 55401
612.455.2294
www.millcitypress.net

ISBN - 1-934248-88-6
ISBN - 978-1-934248-88-1
LCCN - 2008900906

Cover Design and Typeset by James/DZYN Lab

*Printed in the United States of America*

This book is dedicated to my remarkable family,
who have been a never ending source of love

# Angel Writings

On my life's journey, I have had an interesting array of highs and lows common to most of us. I have struggled with anxiety, perhaps, more than many. We each have our own learning in the midst of pain and may be guided to wholeness through these experiences. I feel that my guidance came through these writings from the Divine.

When these writings began, I was most amazed and skeptical as well. I had heard of other's experience with what they felt were remarkable encounters with spiritual events, but I must admit I raised an eyebrow and was somewhat dismissive. I have always been a practical person with a healthy share of cynicism. I certainly did not think I would ever be a candidate for such an experience, yet, I could not explain these writings.

I have sometimes written in a journal before going to sleep, and these writings began to occur at that time. At first, when they remained unsigned, I tried to explain them away thinking I might be using previously "undiscovered enlightenment", (which, even then, I was certain was not the case.) It was a bit unnerving to realize that I had no memory of what was written. My hand just began writing, and not in my handwriting, and my family can attest that I have little affinity for poetic or spiritual writing. These writings were obviously and remarkably different from my emotional rantings and very human outpourings written in my journal.

When I read these writings back to myself, I was amazed that they always spoke to my heart about an emotional issue, difficult event, or troubling encounter which was occurring at that very time. The reference to "wings" and being "surrounded" in early writings which were unsigned appeared significant, and, after a time, these writings began to be signed "Your angels". I began to accept their authorship, and knew that these loving, healing writings were from the Divine.

Recently as I read through these writings which occurred over a period of eight years, I felt these magnificent insights and healing words might help others. A sense of needing to share these writings began to become a voice that would not be silenced.

For publication of these writings, I copied these words in the order given. My heartfelt desire was to present the writings as they were given, to preserve their integrity and meaning. There was, however, no punctuation to show idea endings or beginnings; the pages were simply non-separated words on lines of paper. For easier reading purposes, I made shorter lines, yet added very little punctuation so you might read these words in a way which will speak to your heart. The writings are in chonological order, as received. I omitted names or personal referents and gave my own titles which I felt was a writing's main theme. (Allow that a writing might have quite a different meaning for you.)

As you read these writings, you might need to give yourself time to reread a line or section, but the clarity and understanding will come, as it did with me. I have compiled these writings in an attempt to give back this generous gift which was given to me. My sincere hope is that these profound angel writings might, in some way, enhance your life or help you to heal your heart.

*Nini Finnegan*

# Table of Contents

# Guidelines for Living

Dearest One,
We are near
Go with your heart
Love yourself
Have faith
Trust intuition
Be clear, steady, honest and true
Feel you heart and mind
Clear away scattered things
Be patient and honor life
Take time
Why fret
Know your self
How is easy
Be and do
Beat lightly and feel wonder
Know place
See with an inner eye
Go with life
Attract your good
Bypass head, let the heart beat
Face living
Be graceful
Be in it
Doubts are gone
Give yourself time alone
Be present, be presence

# Healing

Dearest one
The problem is not how but why
See the healing feel the healing
feel the sadness
Be here and know
See visual clarity trust
and know hear the wings
Give up the struggle move slower
We see you whole
No worrying
Embrace the love, the Lover of your soul
Know the Master Healer
Come close and feel the wings

# Pain

Dearest one
The pain will go and spring will come
to your heart and head
Movement will become real
dreams met and fulfilled
No audience, just for you
Not time yet, but soon
Just wait and listen
Healing soon
Winter of your soul is ready for change
We love you

# Upon My Father's Passing

Dearest one
Health is a state of heart
Do your heart
Loved ones passed are in loving hands
No regrets
Love one another
Reach out to people
Loved ones on the other side are waiting
Feel the pain of loss, the way to healing
Eyes cry for good, spirit renewal
We will show you the way to know
what it feels like to purely trust
with knowingness, which is joy
Joy is the absence of all fear

# Happiness

Dearest one
Happiness is yours
Everyday
Seek the experience seek the good
Seek God
Play with the day
Have fun
There's only today
Run and play and laugh
Your family cares
Show them more of your heart
It will heal all hearts

Rest

Dearest one
Rest, rest
Be, be
Go to sleep
Dream
Know the guidance is real
Be under no pressure to get well
Well is a state of heart, mind will follow
Mind will only follow
Mind will only spin, if no heart

# Rest

Dearest one
We love you
You are so special
We feel your family joy
Keep ties with all family
You are being healed slowly and gently
Rest, meditate
Your healing will come
God will use all man-made means
and work with them productively
Rest, rest
You deserve a rest
A renewal is near,
as close as your breathing
Note the wonder of life
Keep seeing minute details
No racing, easy pace with loving

# Anatomic Healing

Dearest one
Body knowing, body knowledge
The spirit in you every tissue,
light in the cells
The cells are filled with white light
You are perfect and whole
Sink into loving yourself
We love you
Feel the wings enfolding you
and feel the mighty Spirit
in the very midst of your body

# Understanding

Dearest one
Look unto the Lord
Don't understand stuff yourself
God is within run through God's filter
The filter of love and joy
with no judgement or fear

# The Gift of Oneself

Dearest one
Feel us, we are so near
Be patient
We are helpers
Come into Spirit and go where you will go
Do not hurry
Flow and reach out
Be ever so kind with yourself
Feel surrounded wherever you go
Feel the gift of yourself
who is confident and strong
Love and joy and enjoyment
comes with passion of what you do
Wanting attracts more wanting
Don't be afraid of wanting and
feel the wonders of your joy

# Discernment

Dearest one
You have been given discernment and
the power to make decisions
easily and with no hardships
We love you and see you moving
the way of your heart
God is here and we love you
Feel the power of the Master's healing hands

# Accepting Help and Wholeness

## Part One

Dearest one
Please accept our help
We will guide you to your good
You must be more still and listen
Spend time with a listening heart
Love your life no matter what is happening
The wind is blowing, healing
Go slow and know the truth
The future will take care of itself
Your life will become a masterpiece
with no effort
Accept your wholeness
Accept your knowledge
Go straight and know that you already know

# Accepting Help
## and Wholeness

Part Two

Let us in
The little girl is so precious
There is no fear here only love
It can be this way there
Accept love
Move slowly for now because the feeling
is new and your feet are too fast for us
When you slow down look in the mirror
and know our love
Honor your own spirit
Go with the eternal God of all
Be a channel of healing

# A Channel for Healing

Dearest one
Be a channel of healing
It is all inside and the light is the opening
Christ light wonderful vast healing energy
It is powerful and will heal because
it is the science of the whole universe
and God is the maker
It is pure love and joy
Joy is freely given
We love you and share your joy
Feel our wings lifting and healing

# On My Daughter

## Part One

Dearest one
Grab your heart
She is pure light and joy
Be with her as we are dancing because
she is the song she is in the song
and can play and or be one with it
She is being sung
by the thousand voices of God
and loving presences
Oh how she is love
and held up and worked through
She sees God, blessed is the joy
that flows and dwells
See your good and call whisper or lift a small
finger and we are there
All the while ever while ever present
and so ready to comfort and laugh
What laughter is bubbling over in all parts of
this lightness this person of completeness
within already coursing through clouds of
joy and fun and greater joy

# On My Daughter

## Part Two

Mother of the free pure spirit of allness
Just allow the being-ness and presence to
find her uncovered with
flowers of beauty and fragrance
There is no burden, maid of goodness, there
is no burden, angel of mercy, compassion,
great joy and purest freest song

# Life Unfolding

Dearest one
This the time to be savored
and loved and deepened
You are on your path of life light
It will be your happiness and happen as its
order unfolds in an abundant and open way
that is your highest wonderment
Be easy and flow
with the colors of the river of life
Take in the blue of healing, the green of peace
and the red of excitement,
and the purple of the divine guidance
There will be not one speck of fear
from us on you as you take us in
It is impossible to fear and love
at the same time
Your abundance and good are yours
and ours and in harmony with all
Feel the all the wholeness
We are ever present
and ever surround you in the Divine joy

# Retirement

Dearest one
Go slow
Know your good
Slower even slower to hear us well
You are to trust and live love and laugh
Trust your love's process
He will always keep you securely grounded
and loved
Ever loving so seeing is he
Listen to his hear of honest and softness
He is safety and love
No need for fear sadness or guilt
They fly away on wings of loving-kindness
No regrets or looks back
or self shame of long ago
It is gone in the sunshine
The long last look
Wind swept clean joyous memories abound
Only joyous past
It is clear
Ledger slate of life is not even kept
No need for sad heart to laugh above
Look over to a new look
A new life

# Flow

## Part One

Dearest one
We are messengers from God
Thanks for listening
It is all within, the abundance
It is not without
You are never without
It is important to release the water of life
which simple and pure just flows
Never does it block, only thoughts do
Your family cherish and love you
Stay close even if nothing
seems close with them
The connect stays open if only you keep it up
The flow is between people, ideas
Your good, prosperity, abundance, desires,
wantings, needings lovings, is all flow
Dance in it and stay in it

# *Flow*

## Part Two

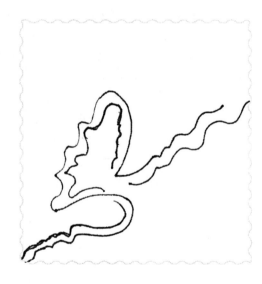

The disconnecting happens when doubt fear
or thoughts of lack interfear with life
so priceless and overwhelming
The price of fear is lack
The lack of love is fear, no flow
Keep the flow unblocked and open and free
and clear and uncluttered and purposeful
We surround your body and we praise your
health and rejoice with you
We are so near with God's love
It is this all knowing presence and spirit
who is guiding you in your journey
Share us too

Your angels

# Easing into the Season

Dearest one
Let your body relax
You will know our presence
and presents, gifts to you
choose the sharing now in letting go
Keep order and feel divinity and flow
There is only the One, the Son, the Father,
the All, the You, the Us
So close is the healing
Give your gift of joy and freedom
of dance and divine expression
Freely give love
Excitement is catching yourself being you
Live in it with serenity and embracement

Your angels

# Christmas and Light

## Part One

Dearest one
Christlight in you is an opening
of abundance joy and love
It comes to you and stays
What joy in heaven
The love is so immense it creates
all you perceive as the truth
We lift you up and hold you
Creative thoughts that come from the heart
Fear is just the confusion of the mind
It stops and clogs and stutters with closed
ideas, with no light or substance
This Christlight is huge unending
with no walls or ceilings
Why dear one would you want to
limit it with stop points
It heals all and can come to any point
in the body temple and work gently
easily and effortlessly
No end, just flow and healing
and perfect stuff
with glowing piercing living light

# Christmas and Light

## Part Two

You can feel our wings soft
and tender from who sent us
The All in All
Jesus is here now
Father is here now
All heavenly bodies are always here now
When you request we overflow with joy

Your Angels

# Allowing Time

## Part One

Dearest one,
Do no fear physical react to your body temple
Feel our flutter wings soft and comfort to you
We love you
Your excitement joy and caring and loving
expectations sometimes carry you to body
feelings which can be mistaken
for images of illness
and there is none
It is illusion which can be fearful
which it is not
Rejoice in your creative mind
It can be too wonderful for words and can
take you across the clouds and to new places
They are there for rejoicing body excitement,
excitation, expectation wonder

# Allowing Time

## Part Two

Slow down to loving-care elation
Slower to peace, joy, acceptance,
growth, calm, healing,
Here is the real healing and joy
which still looks like you
Is the real you
Is the authentic honest-caring
wonder of your spirit
No need to exclude excitation
Embrace it and it will turn
to pure love and flow
Will not stop the flow of
pure joy calm of being
Know the inner not know the outer
Figuring the outer leads to mind thoughts
which are interesting
But not always real
Heart is real
Inclusion of flow embracement
of acceptance are real
Slow the flow to embrace
realness of God's spirit
Christlight is here
Feel His embrace and our wings
Heavenly hosts are with you

# On My Son

Dearest one,
Your feelings toward your child is so loving
He is seeking so hard to find love and joy and
comes the the same exciting place and clouds
his spirit yet brings him closer to it each time
The wonder of new love is such a gift from
God, oh, my Lord of Lords what a gift and he
is blessed these wonders and awash with joy
Oh mother of this wonder-child allow
embrace share these feeling with him
His clouding of his spirit diverts
but also hears his heart
Please feel the help you can get from us
Be in the light and go out and love
Accept other family feelings toward your child
They are sincere wantings to have your child
grow and become himself
Share his loving-kindness
Share your heart with your child and go with
wonder and acceptance

Your angels

# On My Son

## Part One

Dearest one
The answering is here now always
Feel the now-ness newness of spirit
The old fears will fall away
You have such Love for your glorious child
Know that his brokenness will yield
to healing wounds
The end is not the thing
To see the process of living loving spirit will
bring joy and love
to broken hearts and dreams
The processing of loving relationships will
allow nurturing and the miracle of God's love
and daily sharing of gracious thanksgiving
of each other is what your miracle child is
seeking so intensely with eyes wide open
and heart wide open

# On My Son

## Part Two

Don't fear or weep for this intent
is pure of heart tones and lifted
to beautiful choirs through the universe
Go with God adult children of goodness and
love each other with no demand
or any wants to get more
The universal love is there for the taking
Help each other
Take it in
Help each other accept the good
No need to take the small human love to fill
the holes in your soul
You already have it from God, angels,
universe, Jesus and all the heavenly hosts
are there to help
Forever never lean on your own power alone
but let your power mingle with the universe
and feel your lives soar with joy soar with joy
and continuing flying
Always go to the source for your love gap
then share and accept and not fear
and trust the sacred trust your core
No fear, just trust to joy and never ending love

Your angels

# Heart Energy

Dearest one
All energy is continuing
Just making connections is the link
What needs to be in motion will be always
Go with your hearts desire and any act of
creation is why we are here
God loves creation which brings joy
The problems are existing only in your head
Intent will bring success and the knowingness
that things which move will move, will move
And well and perfectly
See it and it is so

Your angels

# Being with the Divine

## Part One

Dearest one
We are here loving your heart
We feel your busy mind
not wanting connection
Let us in to soothe the thinking
Do you feel us
Your trip journey is being prepared slowly
Go forth in love and purpose
Connect with your loved ones
Your dreams will prevail and with ease
No need for apprehension
Appreciation and thanksgiving
is all that is needed
You blessings are here
Come nearer

# Being with the Divine

## Part Two

Love your heart as we do
You are as God
Made of Spirit
Embrace your good
We love you so
Only good comes to you
and remember your good
Doubts are only construction of mind
Creativity is Gods gift
Thankfulness with truth
and honest creates reality
Thank God for your desires
and they will be so
Skepticism for getting true hearts desires is
only illusion and fear
It will all come to you when barriers of
untruths come away
More light is allowed to flow in around
through becoming your true real light

Your angels

# Individual Paths

Dearest one
You are surround with love
Praise your light
Know your good
Compare with no other soul
Souls are made of spirit which are the same
material but infinite in difference
from one to another
All have their own path
Let yours be yours and dance in it
It is only yours
Have incomprehensible mysterious delight
in your life
Your abundance is enormous
What joy you bring
No road blocking when you keep a view on
your path of infinite love and joy

Your angels

# Energy, Flow and Ullness

Dearest one
You are finding what makes you ill
Too much push
You know that no more effort is needed
Even if more busy is there
The slower, easier you go
the more energy, moving, flow
will center and be with your spirit
Keep your spirit in tune with easy flow
God sent energy, airy movement
This energy is purposeful but not intense
It has intent and design but no intensity
All that is needed is done
and nothing more is needed
God/Spirit direct and perform

Your angels

# What Is Your Life Idea?

## Part One

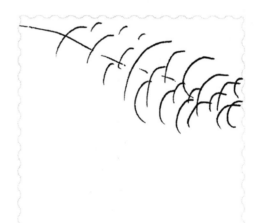

Dearest one
Peace is with you listening to God
It is always coming to you
just open your eyes and ears
Are you doing your life idea?
Not doing anything, doing something, being
you, living, breathing, experiencing lovingness
are doing your life idea
What a gift to share your light love
and be seen to you and old hearts
The glow is who you are
the after burning of life presence
Knowing this no talk is needed of life journey
You are it, it is you
and it is glorious in the living
Whatever else is there?
These questions of paths to choose are not
answered because any choice is the good
Any choice is the joy
If the pressing in is felt then allow it to ease
Then it too is wonderful

# What Is Your Life Idea?

## Part Two

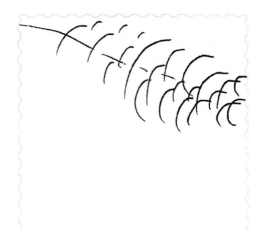

Time stretching is a choice
you do yet we help you
So the stretching works well
It may not be necessary to do this intensive
stretching and your pain is felt
when time seems too small for you
The remembering here
is that there is always plenty of time
Do you remember
It is not short or small there is always enough
if the concentration is on the ease
and joy of it
Life experience is missed if stretching
moments are not felt and tasted

Your angels

# Health

## Part One

Dearest one
Let it go
Let all tight feeling body parts go
down to no tense body or ideas thoughts
Let the love feeling warm through you
The greatest presence is opening within
Feel the light
What holds the dis-ease is the mind
All are one just spirit/soul
The film of life, the force, the special
separate, yet unite spirit
Health is the same as not health, just the
perception changes what we choose to learn
from remembering
There are reasons to not choose health
We can remember from the dark side as
much as the light side

# Health

Part Two

No need to analyze health
none will come of such
Just open and wait for the heart to hear
Open, open ears, eyes,
heart with a reborn-ness
A feel for new sight of new light
The dark side of health
is only in the perceiving
Find different routes to health goals
The thought, the way,
the place is already here
No new learnings, just rememberings
Seek with a feeling of such love
of your own soul and body temple
What you see of your body is not all there is
It is also within
All seeking of health is within
Listen to your breath
Feel the strength within
It is all for the taking

# Health

## Part Three

The waiting will encourage patience
and joy in the very doing of health
There is nothing our Source wants more
than free souls
The taking and the knowing of the good
The taking and knowing
of how good your good is
is the true knowing
There is nothing to fear
in the healing of the free soul
All is yours and is granted freely
No history of any other
is important to your healing
Only the pieces of perception
that you want to include
You are being healed are healed
at this very moment
All is well

Your angels

# Healing: Life & Death

## Part One

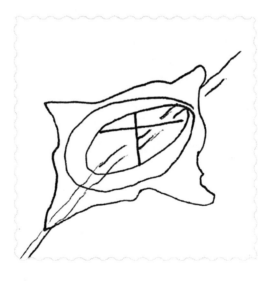

Dearest one
We are still here listening and comforting
What about the death or discard
of the body temple
It is simply that
The soul/spirit lives forever
Jesus knew, many know
You know and all is needed
is the remembering
What of the pain of transition
Perception of the knowing
that all is within, is all
Nothing is without when you know within
The opening to healing is complete when the
heart and soul are willing to allow all in
The fighting or blocking against pain
causes the suffering
Let the window to your heaven open
Heaven here on earth

# Healing: Life & Death

## Part Two

Now and forever
there is no separation only joy
We can hear it over and over again is the
perception of all, is what it is
Whether pain or any other, the healing is
in the remembering of the unity of Spirit,
Source, body, the whole tree,
the all in all,
It is all within
There is no separation
Know that your are healed

# *Healing: Life & Death*

## Part Three

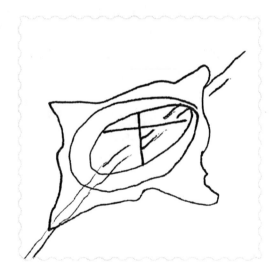

Fear is only the opposite of love
Fear is not even an interesting choice
because there is no need
no use no reason to have it
In the drama of our lives
only brightness and beauty are significant
and fear has no room
although ever so human
The passion and light of the Christ within
only needs remembering
Use it dearest one

Your angels

# On Relationship

## Part One

Dearest ones
Feel the joy of your union
Delight in one another
Know each is a rose of great beauty
Delicate sensitive
and the be cherished and loved
Feel our presence feel our presence and
listen trust, trust,
trust each others spirit to relate in love
No fear of abandonment or deception will
prevail when love and trust abound
See the rose of great beauty
and tenderness within
Protect each others sensitivity so the petals
and leaves remain and flourish
Know and delight in the knowledge
that there is forever

# On Relationship

## Part Two

A seeming conflict is not when listened to
carefully given time and space
Find the quiet space within before proceeding
with harmful words
The seeming conflict is not
The seeming conflict is not when looked at
with open eyes ears and hearts with trust and
love and when given time and space and the
allowing in of our angel wings
Allow us in
Love God and soft angel wings and the caring
You are so loved
You are so loved
You are constantly loved and cared for oh
lovers of the heart
And great help is within the listening caring

# On Relationship

## Part Three

Reach out at all times
Don't lean on your own understanding when
old wounds and the wanting to be right
seems to keep bubbling up
These wounds can be healed easily and
effortlessly in listening to your hearts with the
Divine to comfort and surround you
Allow each other the expanse of time for
each others healing
Demand will kill trust and demands will allow
the rose to wither and die
Demands are only fear and lack of trust
See the light of precious souls

# On Relationship

## Part Four

Never worry if the same difference between
souls appear to arise again and again
It is just your souls trying to heal
It is all illusion as soon as the greater love is
seen when the beauty of each others delicate
sensitve rose petals are honored
and loved and trusted
Trust in your beauty soul
Trust in each others soul of beauty and honor,
love and protect each other in the knowing
that you have forever
to grow in understanding
You have forever to find greater joy
You have forever to know each other
and dear ones you will delight in taking every
moment of time
There is no right way
Only the way of love

Your angels

# Your Child Within

## Part One

Dearest one
All you have is caring
Give your love to someone who cares and
feels the same loving kindness
Open to new loves, lovers of the soul
You have the friendships all around
Know they love you and give yourself freely
and don't make corners of yourself which hurt
The wounds of the childhood are deep
When you were young you didn't know the
secure heart within
When you grew up
you do now know these things
But the child-heart still is waiting to be heard
healed and loved not knowing
that it already is
The grown up heart it will take your child
by the hand and heal it

# Your Child Within

## Part Two

The child is wanting to love, live without
restriction
The way has appeared hard but is not
Her way is still appearing hard
and laborious but is not
The perceiving through child eyes
is clouding the way
The pursuit of the knowing through the mind
only is a strenuous difficult way
And with child wounds is even more so

# Your Child Within

## Part Three

The knowing through the mind is too difficult
Real knowing is knowing through the heart
The heart knowing is only remembering
Oh child within hear us
No strain is needed
Take joy in the helping
You are not any more than a helping hand
when you can or want
Nothing more is needed
Let this now swirl and land where it will
and let it go
And accept with loving kindness
her good as it is shown
Feel the petals on your cheek
from the lovers of your soul

Your Angels

# Feeling Betrayal

## Part One

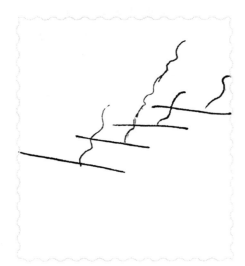

Dearest one
Now let go
It is not yours it is ours
It is Gods
When will you give it all up
It is now it is now
Breathe it out
Inhale, exhale
You cannot gain or breathe
when you hold on
Give it all over
It is gone not to be held
The holding will hurt you
Let it go yes give it up
There is no head control it is illusion
Only heart love
Feel the power of clear running love
through the heart
It doesn't see the flaws
or path of another
It doesn't want anything
because it is already here for you
Go with your heart and say nothing
Nothing of others failings or mistakes

# Feeling Betrayal

## Part Two

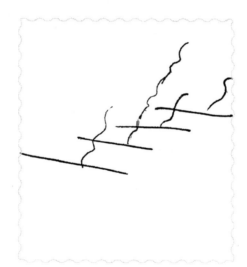

Cry out for your justices
but know you can see clearer when
Your eyes are on your passions of the heart
Not others flaws
Your block in your eye is huge too
It is blocking so defenses remain up
against hurt and pain
The pain is past
The pain of no honesty deceit
secrets not sharing
But all is swept away and the block in the
dam can gush forth and heal the hurt and run
you along the path of love
Let the light shine with ever widening wonder
Watch it and run with it
Feel it
Let the dam of tears break forth and heal
All dis-ease will fall away and the joy of the
community of lovers will survive and run free
Hear us, here us

Your angels

# Being Wronged

## Part One

Dearest one
Cry for the child who abandoned the soul
You felt there was no inside help
It wasn't trusted
Remember how loved
and revered your heart is
Always remember your heart with no fear
It will serve you with joy and love
Our joy and your joy is complete with love
and confidence that strength of character
and understanding
The pain of confronting a wrong
is only fear of no love
The wrong is wrong
No need for self doubt
Trust your inside soul and trust in God
Inside this idea of light
In the center is real and so right

# Being Wronged

## Part Two

Know that you are loved and revered
Your light is in every cell
Enter into this with a clean heart
Let the fear sparkle and transform
into more joy
Keep open and expand
and it is perfect
Let the sun in
Let God and all angels in which is perfect love
The fear is very old and will transform with
the trusting of your heart
God light is inside of your every cell
Let it out and feel the room
It will fit in any space at all
It will crowd out any wrong

Your angels

# Feeling Emptiness

Dearest one
The emptiness you feel
is an opening to your newness of life
The hole is pain at rebirth
Some more of the sad child
is going to become real and whole
See the hole
It is not black but new and green with vines
and flowers blooming ready to open
It is the fear of the new
the change that obscures
It is truly ready for your touching and ready to
explode into understanding
Embrace your good
Your God
It is not that you must change and grow
It is just that you will

Your angels

# On My Daughter

## Part One

Dearest one
You are like the sun, much too bright, shiny
And is hard to make such a huge mark in time
and space as you do
What you are is not what you do
No need to keep going at such a pace
Enjoy the life/light and love your self joyfully
Your spirit lightly touches the earth unless
weighed down with doubt
It is so strong to experience
your soul when weight is here
Be with your God within
and love all of yourself
Be aware of the loving arms
Do not struggle for words
Just let it be
All choices are good with the light
Be ever so light in the light

# On My Daughter

## Part Two

Illness will pass
and can be a teacher of wellness
Feel our wing fluttering presence
God is within
Know you are surrounded
with his love and ours
Feel the lifting of the illusion of illness
This lifting is the healing of mind
and body so needed for joy
The veil has covered
but it is not the natural state
It is lifting
Cry for the child within
who hasn't yet felt the wings lifting
Then the tears will wipe even the fears away
Tears of joy and love
You do not have to prove
your loving soul anymore
Just do your heart
All are acts of love

Your angels

# Guilt

## Part One

Dearest one
We are trying to come
Guilt is an illusion
and is creating a wall of tightness
Let it go to the Lord God on high
of the universe
Guilt is not yours dear one
it is only a wall of the mind
Go to your heart made of love because God,
Good is there and is the very love you seek
The guilt wall is cracking now
Feel the lightness in your heart
No decision is wrong or unchangeable
Be with your beauty of caring
The caring will come no matter
because of your God,
Good loving heart
This heart of light is not an illusion
Guilt and fear are illusions
There is no room for them

# Guilt

## Part Two

Open your eyes to the reality
of the everlasting love
Go in beauty and light
We say God's love never stops
You are forgiven without the asking because
there is nothing to forgive
These decisions or acts which cause you pain
will be lifted away with the incoming of the
Christlight the Godlight the Light of the world
The pain is the remembrance
of the small child you were
Not the remembrance of the spirit/soul
In remembering who you are and what your
spirit is made of
There is no cognition of guilt

# Guilt

## Part Three

We lift these burdens from you dearest one
We know that they aren't of your true spirit
Your mind does not need any more play
Only your spirit/soul
Let the universal mind, the big mind,
the Lord God of all
take away the guilt and understand
completely the pain
Let it go let it go
We will hover and be near you
You will feel the light
Feel the glow and warmth
Good night dear one
Learn and hear and feel us as you sleep

Your angels

# Blame / Shame

Dearest one
We are around you
Feel our wings
See the sky and wonders of nature
The natural
No need for words
What makes you feel so responsible
No one is required to take the yoke of guilt
No judgements will come
The illness you have is real
yet you can see its illusion
The illness is your burdon of the yoke
Let it go
There is no pointing
the sharp finger of blame/shame
You no longer need them
Head illness is head illness
Give up the holding
Let it whisper daily, hourly all any every time
to flow freely flow freely give
Be in love with your soul and you will soar
and give back without thinking/knowing
No counting and no accounting
Love is yours and always has been
Just remember

Your angels

# Your Peace / Your Place

## Part One

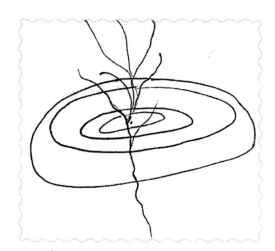

Dearest one
You are so loved
We know your heart
We love your soul
Your need for peace peaceful surroundings
Peace surrounds you every where
You can stand in lifes fires
yet your can choose lifes peace
Both all and other choices
are there for the choosing
Changes which stir the spirit
are simply that
To not be feared
Flow with the spirit of love
in all you do
Be your spirit
Conflicts with your peace are not
Just choose the other road
Road noise can hinder

# Your Peace / Your Place

## Part Two

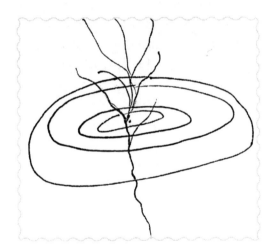

We are made to choose
what our creative idea of peace is
Listen and your place will come
and your peace will come
Be in your place and stand in your spirit
Feel the comfort overjoy and over flow
If your place no longer overjoys
Your place can move
Let the energy of your spirit take it
where it will go
Stand in your place
because it always is there
even when moving
Stand in your place
Stand in your peace

Your angels

# *Partner*

## Part One

Dearest one
You are pure love and joy
Find your complete joy and peace
There is time and space for all to happen
easily and with no effort or pain
Let all abide in joy
Exclude the string of fear
The beads are redundance and untrue
Let go of the strand and the beads of worry
tension and dis-ease are gone too
There are unfairnesses yet trust
Trust your wonderful love
and companion to understand your place
This love will help you to stand in your place
where you are being you

# *Partner*

## Part Two

Be open kind forgiving and loving as you open
your spirit to your love, your lover
Your partner is such a lover of your soul and
dancer with your spirit
Remember that you have all you need within
The God of all is within and part of the all in all
Rejoice in this omniscience
Be still and allow the workings
Be still and know our good will manifest

Your Angels

# Abundance

## Part One

Dearest one
Let us love you freely and completely
Fill every part with wholeness
We are complete in you and you are
completely whole in us
Open to the brilliance of the light
Be filled so completely to every cell that
worries about finances and material things or
supposed bad decisions are not
No one can take your source,
your spirit, your love, your joy
No one, no thing, no power
You are you and have all the abundance you
want and so much more
There is a universe and eternity
A never ending supply
You limit the horizon which goes on forever
Your abundance is here in front of you already

# Abundance

## Part Two

Share yourself
The gift the love of God to all you meet
It keeps coming back
and all others will be added
All will keep being added
with no request and no thought of such
If it were not so we would have told you
You know the truth and you are free
The truth is the abundance that surrounds you
Reach out or even not
Let it come and whisper and show itself
Feel our presence and the universal gifts
and outpouring never ends
We love you so
We love the world and give these gifts to all
even amidst the crying and sadness
All the souls have lifted and have created a
choir of hundreds of angels
and love spirit to heal the worlds wounds
So much more is seen now
Love to you and your family
and the family of man

Your angels

# Inter-Relationships

## Part One

Dearest one
There is only one Source
You cannot be the One
You can love without judgment
You can be one with the One, but not the One
God is inside outside omniscient
every where all the time
Being present feeling presence at every
moment opens the door
Love flows freely and you are love
You can mirror the love
Be present be presence
The One presence works through
Let the wings be heard through you
Let the light be seen through you
You be the light
but not the carrier of the burdon
Lift up friends and family
Look at the love flowing like a feather floating
down slowly and it is on meandering time
It is going where it needs to go

# Inter-Relationships

## Part Two

Stay in the present
in the presence throughout your day
Your interactions your meetings your
serendipities all are exactly right
Relationships are exactly right
for you to learn dear one
Reawaken to the spirit, your spirit
Your true spirit, your warm, friendly, easy
flowing light soul, light universal light with
such special light combines for power
Fears of relationships, being not liked or not
included are nothing but illusion
Your future will unfold in the present presence
It is here now so there is no fear
The fear is over and never was
The time is here
Time future is not
Be here with us
We love you so stay in the truth

Your Angels

# Regrets

## Part One

Dearest one
It is not so hard
if seen through present eyes
Stay here now
Feel the life flowing through you
Relationship is just you with a mirror
Look to the mirror and see your spirit
Stay with your spirit
and other spirits who you love will stay or go
The flow will happen
through acceptance of nonjudgement
Happiness cannot be disguised
Know your happiness
It is here easily
Nothing is hard that is not forced
Let it flow let love flow or go if it needs to
Settle somewhere else
Nothing is lost
Loving is not lost
Letting go is not lost
Fear will only ever be shown as an illusion
It will flow and go if left unimpaired

# Regrets

## Part Two

Guilt, fear, anger, judgement all flow over
and are released when truth of spirit see light
and are allowed to grow open
Open to light and love
and stinging sticky fear will go
Let it up
There is no need to explain or keep it stuck by
more thoughts and words
Nothing is lost dear one
There are no regrets just tears for growing
The letting go of layers
and layers of covering of the soul
which thinks itself not good enough
The spirit is all so beautiful
No losses even in losses
Tears for other spirits
which need to grow differently
No thought no regret no anguish
Let it up dear one
Relationship will come back or go gently

Your angels

# Anguish & Control

Dearest one
Are you feeling anguish?
Let it bubble up to heal the spirit
You can learn from the shadow side
Look at the shadow side
It will help you to walk
Bubbles of healing are coming up
to make you whole
These bubbles are not to be feared
Just acknowledged and made friendly
The bubbles are new and seem
to make you feel
Out of control
When control has been a lifeline
It feels so different to be out of control
It is exactly where your spirit needs to be
It is reopening reacquainting
remembering itself
In its beauty
Love the bubbles even
though they feel shadowy
The bottom becomes the top
once seen with new eyes
The emergence of the spirit is all there is
No going back
to the illusion of control and fear
Stay with spirit holy one

Your angels

# Warrior Spirit

Dearest one
The one you are is who you are
The healing you ask for is spiritual
is the healing of your
Spirit and soul
You connect with other souls
and feel their pain and it is so
Overwhelming and strong
that your spirit blocks it
Yet it also can block all the good
the God the Joy the
Source the Essence
The healing and strength you seek
is this Good, God,
Source, Essence
Open to Spirit open to God
with no fear of being
Overwhelmed overpowered
or losing your essence
All essences connect dear warrior
and protector
Know the connections
Welcome the brotherhood of all
It never means becoming like,
or being taken in
The one you are is who you are
Love your spirit as we love you

Your angels

# Change

## Part One

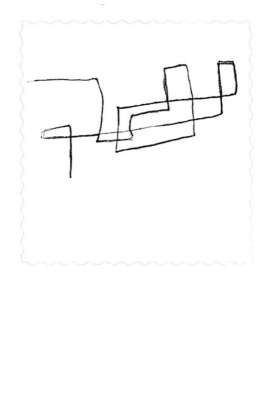

Dearest one
The fear you feel
you understand as an illusion
It can be used to tap our comfort every day
It comes with changes and
big shifts in your position in your life on earth
Come to us oh precious and loved one
Be with us for comfort
God loves you so all changes are good
You will be protected and easy in your new
life
It will feel free and open and new experiences
will come your way
And you will greet them with the serendipity
which they possess

# Change

## Part Two

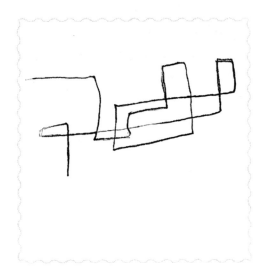

None is not welcomed or by chance
It is in the great scheme of things
that your life unfolds
Greet each new challenge with lightness
and the freedom which
They possess
We love you so only good
will be with the changes
Points of sparkle and excitement
You can be ever so calm in their coming
Our wings flutter and surround their coming
Our Lord is with us all
to usher in the newness
See the good in all for the coming is good
We love you so much dearest
and most precious one

Your angels

# Thanksgiving

Dearest one
Be with your family this Thanksgiving Day
All have sparks of joy and light
and you need not be the head planner
We love to be included
Include accept open to our love and joy
We will be in every moment and your entire
family will too
God bless this time of joy

Your angels

# Ulness

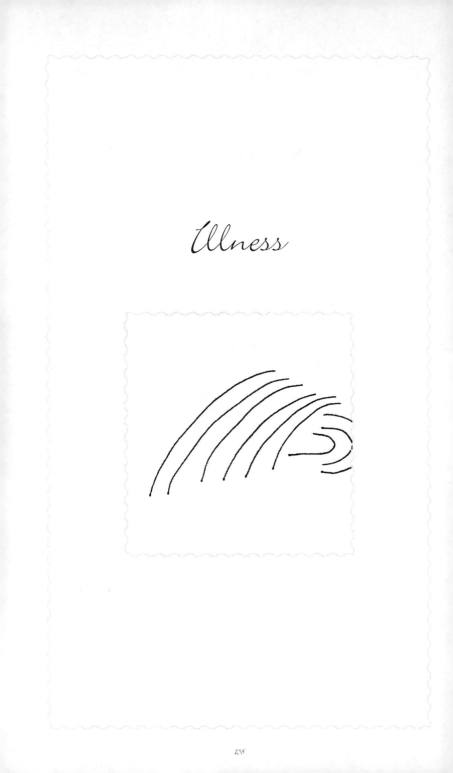

Dearest one
You ask about your illness
We are close for your comfort
All acknowledge for your healing is within
Your vibrating is good
The eveness of the light and circling is the
trying to heal
Perceive all as moving toward the healing
Let the light move through
No stopping or thought of not healing
The way is slow and clean
The way is unwavering and pure
Increase the breath
Decrease the thought
Follow the moving light that is God
It is available and so loving
Your spirit is filling
Is filled
See you light and good
Be still with your spirit
Be still and feel see be in the moving light of
love joy and happiness
No fear of future
Be with yourself and love the light
Move with and in it

Your angels

# Belonging

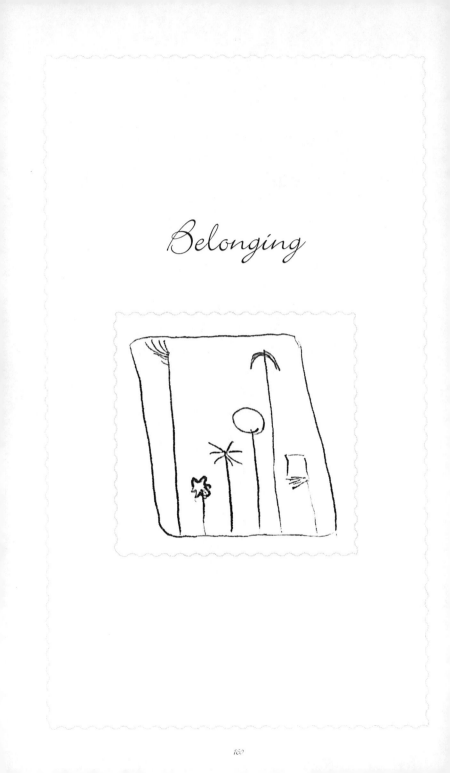

Dearest one
Invite your loving people into your heart
Sing play move into the Lord
We hear your cry for community
Trust the gathering in Gods name
The community of believers is you and you
are part and not alone
Rejoice
Rejoice in your gifts to share and theirs
Your church is within as well as without
Trust and accept love
Oh spirit of life and love
The place is already here and now
Go with your heart
Listen
Time to listen time to hear
Feel your own sanctuary
Know your path
Listen and flow
Sense belonging

Your angels

# Your Path

Dearest one
Your healing is here
Enjoy the feeling and goodnesses
A wonderful light is within and without
Believe and open to the light
Your decisions will be easy and effortless
when you let them mingle
With the light
It can permeate all being
It will make the crooked roads
clear and straight
Your path will be made clear
Your path is clear
It is only the shroud of doubt that confuses
Trust in the process of love and light
It flows in and through everything
See the light and love in others and in
seeming disturbing events
All paths will sparkle with clarity
Do not impair your journey-decision
with doubt
It will happen oh so easily and effortlessly
with love and joy
Be the joy
You spread it so freely
Do what you are
Be what you are
Soak in the light
Spread your being

Your angels

# Open Your Spirit

## Part One

Dearest one
Love who you are
No fear of spreading love
Do nothing to hide your spirit
It bubbles and it continues to bubble
and pop and sparkle and twinkle
It is OK to be and feel your wonderful self
We hold up all that is true and joy filled
See the Christlight
The face of compassion in all of life
To be compassionate is your awakening
To laugh and be joy is the journey of love
life of your love and life
Helping children see themselves
is a window
Do such good works
We will be as mirrors to our children
You children are seekers
and a soul calling for itself
You are part of their journey
We are all parts to support the whole
There is no fear from the outcome
of looking out for one another
Just help and holding up and seeing the
Christ in all

# Open Your Spirit

## Part Two

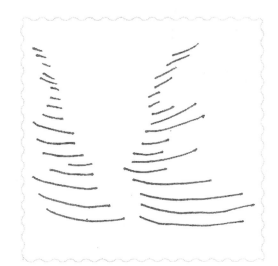

Christ compassion
Christ joy Christ love
The heart of the Christ is the joy to emulate
The model of compassion one to another
There is no owner or possessor
of one another
No one who is the only responsible care
provider because the other is
the God self already
The other to be supported is already whole
Sometimes it takes only a mirror
to reflect what is already is
It might also be a word or sound or gesture
or face that might reflect a path
For the other the children the family
Let the other soul float toward the light with
illumination from your mirrors and windows
Stand along the way to hold them firm
We love you so

Your angels

Printed in the United States
126424LV00002B/1-99/P